—THE—
ENNEAGRAM
TYPE 6
journal

A Guide to Inner Work & Self-Discovery
for The Loyalist

THIS JOURNAL BELONGS TO:

Published in the United States by: Hay House LLC: www.hayhouse.com®
Published in Australia by: Hay House Australia Publishing Pty Ltd: www.hayhouse.com.au
Published in the United Kingdom by: Hay House UK Ltd: www.hayhouse.co.uk
Published in India by: Hay House Publishers (India) Pvt Ltd: www.hayhouse.co.in

Cover design: Julie Davison
Interior design: Lisi Mohandessi
Author photo: Courtesy of Deborah Threadgill Egerton, Ph.D.

Tradepaper ISBN: 978-1-4019-7906-5
10 9 8 7 6 5 4 3 2 1
1st edition, May 2024

This product uses responsibly sourced papers and/or recycled materials. For more information, see www.hayhouse.com.

Printed and bound by CPI Group (UK) Ltd, Croydon, CR0 4YY

MIX
Paper | Supporting
responsible forestry
FSC® C013604

THE
ENNEAGRAM
TYPE 6
journal

DEBORAH THREADGILL EGERTON, Ph.D.
& LISI MOHANDESSI

HAY HOUSE LLC
Carlsbad, California • New York City
London • Sydney • New Delhi

This journal is dedicated to
Norman Y. Mineta.
Role model and mentor.
Activists and friend.
We will see you on
the other side.

You are gifted with a body that allows you to be here in the present moment, a mind that opens access to unlimited possibilities to be explored, and a heart that holds the enormous capacity to love and be loved.

This is the authentic you. You will find yourself when you accept the beauty of your true nature.

Gratitude for who you are is the first step.

Grace will follow.

Caritas,
Deborah & Lisi

CONTENTS

Enjoy your journey, and
may you find love and
light within yourself.

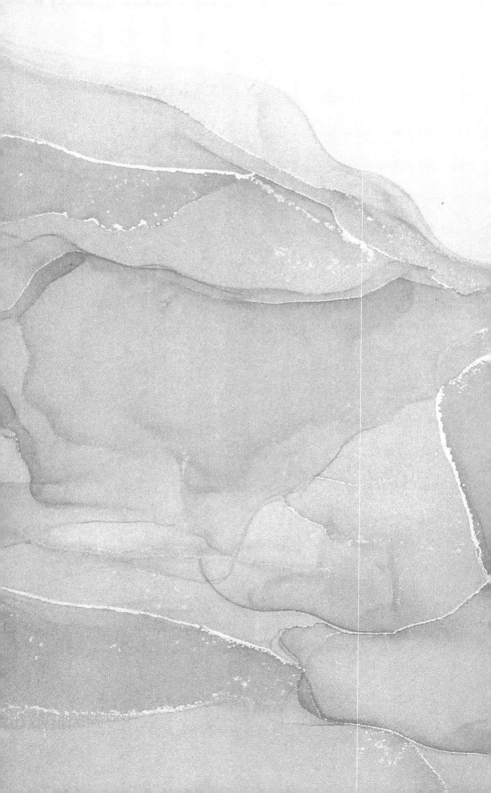

INTRODUCTION

Many of us journey through life pondering the reasons behind our actions and how we can enrich our lives. We seek not only improvement but also a sense of tranquility, productivity, and purpose. Conversations with friends, colleagues, mentors, and partners often echo the advice to "do the work." This phrase never fails to elicit a knowing smile because if it were that simple, we would already be immersed in the process of "doing the work." Yet we continually find ourselves returning to the fundamental question: What is the work?

A deep understanding of oneself is necessary to live a life brimming with abundance, creativity, joy, and love. Self-awareness is a journey inward, a voyage to explore how we present ourselves to the world, and the Enneagram will serve as our guide. Clues about our true selves are sometimes scattered before us, but we often choose to look away from anything that challenges our self-image. This is why the voyage inward, toward self-realization, becomes indispensable in uncovering our genuine, authentic selves.

This journal is thoughtfully crafted to accompany you on this very journey as you harness the insights of the Enneagram. Within these pages you'll encounter an array of writing prompts, mindfulness exercises, inspirational quotes, and grounding meditations for introspection. Each page is a deliberate step along your unique path. It's crucial to remember that this process cannot be hurried or coerced. Guidance on this voyage comes from a source known by many names—God, the Universe, the Divine, Spirit, or a name entirely personal to your experience. All these concepts are interconnected. You need not adhere to any dogmatic religious structure; what truly matters is connecting with that part of you that acknowledges a higher force, shaping and influencing your choices and your path forward.

This journal isn't something you casually dip into; rather, it's an invitation to cultivate a consistent habit of exploring its pages, allowing you to fully embrace the practices within. These pages are designed to guide you toward a profound understanding of why you do what you do.

The Enneagram stands out as a radiant gem among the many personality typing systems, and it beckons with a warm, unique approach centered on uncovering motivations rather than mere behaviors. It opens a doorway to explore the why behind our actions, inviting us to discover the roots of our behaviors. As we delve into this exploration, we find newfound flexibility, unlocking exciting possibilities we may have never imagined before.

We encourage you to delve deeper into the understanding of your dominant Enneagram energy, which is akin to picking up a mirror to gaze upon yourself in a way you've never done before. The idea may initially seem a bit intimidating, but the richness of your life is directly linked to the depth you're willing to explore within your soul.

Your life inherently possesses meaning, purpose, and a trajectory leading toward goodness; it's our natural inclination. Sometimes, we find ourselves needing to reconnect with what truly matters. We might start to wonder and feel disoriented when we sense that we've drifted away from our guiding light. But remember, that guidance hasn't abandoned us; it's possible we've simply strayed from it, unable to see what's right in front of us.

As you embark on this journey, we wish you all the goodness and benefits it has to offer. It's not about reaching a final destination but about following your guiding light, aligning yourself with what's genuine, trustworthy, and good in both the world and within yourself. Return to the pages of this journal daily, allowing your journey to inform you and lead you toward truth, joy, love, light, and goodness. All these elements reside within you, and they'll never abandon you. Sources of love and joy perpetually surround us, and by embracing the truth of goodness in the world, you'll radiate with the light found inside yourself.

This journal is designed as your reference guide and exploratory workbook. The following section will gently guide you through the Enneagram system and provide an overview of Type Six energy. Within these pages, you'll find a wealth of knowledge about the Enneagram; and using this journal is a chance to reignite your inner connection with your Enneagram Six energy. Prepare yourself, for your mind will be engaged, your heart will be touched, and your body will respond; all of these experiences, both uplifting and challenging, are an integral part of the journey. We hope you continue to revisit these pages as you further your journey deeper into the Enneagram system.

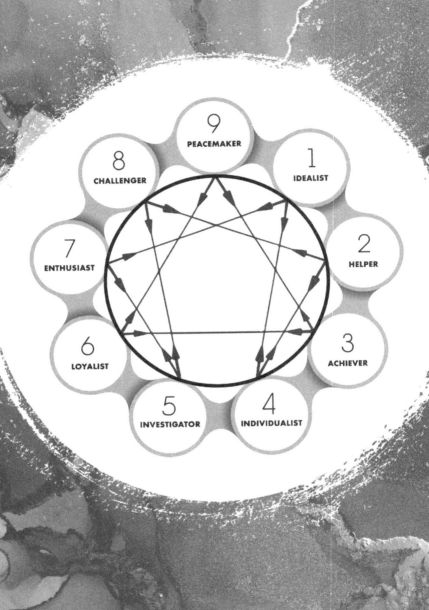

The Enneagram

The Enneagram is an archetypal personality system that combines modern psychological practices with a deep foundation in ancient traditions, religions, cultures, and spiritual practices. It is a model of the human psyche taught as a typology of nine personality archetypes. These types have names that reflect the nine different energies: Eight, Challenger; Nine, Peacemaker; One, Idealist; Two, Helper; Three, Achiever; Four, Individualist; Five, Investigator; Six, Loyalist; and Seven, Enthusiast.

The Enneagram invites you to embark on a journey of self-discovery, unlocking the intricate mechanisms governing your existence. It allows you to delve into the why behind your actions and the how of your daily functioning in pursuit of fulfilling your needs. Unveiling your core motivations, values, fears, and inherent strengths is a perpetual source of insight. Simultaneously, the Enneagram casts light on the egoic patterns that occasionally hinder our progress, thwarting our alignment with our true selves. More significantly, while this insightful system aids us in uncovering our authentic selves, it equally guides us in connecting with others, fostering appreciation, and cultivating genuine presence.

This beginning section is designed to serve as a refresher on the basics of the Enneagram and a quick look into each of the nine types. Remember: the Enneagram is a fluid system that provides access to all nine types, and we encourage you to explore your relationship with all of these energies.

The moment you intentionally chose to use this journal, you began your journey to discover who you really are instead of creating another version of yourself. Or, as people like to say, "the best version of yourself." Your goal now is to find out who you are underneath all the versions of yourself that you have created. Welcome to the journey of your lifetime! May you find joy, peace, acceptance, and belonging in this exploration. May love be your path, and may light shine on every step you take. Most importantly, may you fall deeply in love with the authentic you. The glorious being that you were created to be.

A QUICK OVERVIEW OF THE BASICS OF THE ENNEAGRAM

TYPE/POINT

Each of the nine Enneagram points possesses unique energies and characteristics. When discussing an Enneagram type, we are identifying the specific point on the Enneagram where one embodies the most significant energy. It's important to note that we have access to all nine points on the Enneagram, each contributing to our holistic understanding and personal growth.

CENTERS OF INTELLIGENCE

The Enneagram is explored through three Centers of Intelligence: Body, Heart, and Head. Sometimes, these centers, or triads, are called Body/Instinctive, Heart/Feeling, and Head/Thinking. Each center has a connection to particular emotions: the Body, anger and rage (Eight, Nine, One); the Heart, shame and guilt (Two, Three, Four); and the Head, fear and anxiety (Five, Six, Seven).

BASIC DESIRE AND BASIC FEAR

We all have inner drive and internalized fear that affect all of our behaviors, beliefs, and actions. You may resonate with all nine basic fears and desires, as we are beings composed of all nine energies; however, you will have the most substantial connection to one corresponding fear and desire of one specific type.

CORE MOTIVATION

The core motivation constantly challenges us to get what we most desire at any given moment while avoiding what we fear that will cause our demise. The core motivation is your internal drive, the reason you wake up in the morning, how you navigate life, and that thing that gets you going or paralyzes you. Think of the core motivation as why you do what you do.

WINGS

The types on either side of your dominant Enneagram energy affect how your type shows up in the world. Every Enneagram type has two wings; however, one of the wings may significantly influence the energy of your dominant Enneagram type.

LINES AND ARROWS

The Enneagram lines and arrows, also referred to as the stress and security points or directions of growth and stress, connect the types across the map. There are multiple ways of using the lines and arrows when we see them as connections to pick up specific qualities at specific times. We can move freely between these connections, picking up positive and negative energies as we need them to create a warning system and a path for growth.

PASSION: THE WAY WE SUFFER — PERSONAL CHALLENGE

The passions represent the nine main ways we lose our center, become more susceptible to personality distortions, and become disoriented from reality. We can refer to each of the passions as the way in which each type suffers.

FIXATION: HOW WE GET STUCK — THE TRAP

We all have a way of becoming trapped in our personality, which we see play out through the fixation. These "traps" are mental blocks we hold on to when attempting to justify our reality.

VIRTUE: OUR TRUE NATURE — THE GIFT

Honoring our true selves and who we become develops when we land in our virtue. These specific characteristics manifest through the emotional awareness of the authentic self, and the letting go of ego, self-deception, and dynamic vices. When we access our virtue, we become selfless and altruistic in our actions, feelings, and beliefs.

INSTINCTS

The Instincts, sometimes referred to as Subtypes and Instinctual Variants, within each Enneagram energy are Self-Preservation, Social, and Sexual (sometimes referred to as One-on-One). The Instincts can be mirrored in the three drives for survival: preserving life and focusing on physical needs, mutual cooperation and creating social bonds, and species survival through exploration and experiencing energies. We have a dominant instinct that we feel most comfortable with and a secondary instinct to support the dominant one. The third instinct is usually the least developed, therefore, an area that manifests as an unseen personal challenge.

LEVELS OF DEVELOPMENT

The Levels of Development established by Don Riso and Russ Hudson demonstrate the varying degrees of how each type can show up in the world based on presence. Healthy, average, and unhealthy refer to the Levels of Development and the overall state of a person's ability to function. The energy of each type can show up very differently depending on how healthy or unhealthy the individual is; this is a common reason why many people mistype or feel uncomfortable as their dominant type.

Healthy—Becoming expansive and unconstricted in essence, fully present in the world

Average—Beginning to allow our egos to guide our behaviors, dropping into destructive patterns when we fall asleep to our true selves, with a fluctuation of presence

Unhealthy—Dysfunctional and destructive behaviors when ego becomes the driving force behind everything we do; falling into ego-based patterns that trap us in personality

HEALTHY	L1	BEING	Freedom from Ego Structure
	L2	ALLOWING	Psychological Capacity ("I Am")
	L3	DOING	Social Value / Gift
AVERAGE	L4	EFFORTING	Social Role / Imbalance
	L5	IMPOSING	Interpersonal Control
	L6	AGGRESSION	Overcompensation
UNHEALTHY	L7	VIOLATING	Violation
	L8	COMPULSIVE	Delusion & Compulsion
	L9	DESTROYING	Pathological Destruction

ADAPTED FROM THE RISO-HUDSON LEVELS OF DEVELOPMENT

THINGS TO REMEMBER

- There are nine points on the Enneagram map. We can access all the points but lead with one dominant type. The numbers are not a scale, meaning no type is better or worse than any other type. However, in order to keep the Enneagram energies grouped by the centers of intelligence, we look at the types in this order: Eight, Nine, One, Two, Three, Four, Five, Six, Seven.

- Your dominant Enneagram type does not change throughout your life or shift based on your home or work life. You are born into your type, and your experiences adjust how you navigate life, access your wing energy, travel with the arrows, and drop into the Levels of Development.

- No type is inherently gendered or dependent on dimensions of diversity (perceived race, socioeconomic status, education, age, religion, etc.). While the descriptions and energies of the types are universal and are not dependent on certain identifying factors, it is essential to note how an Enneagram energy can vary based on cultural or environmental influences or psychological well-being. For instance, some cultures have specific gender roles, socially acceptable values, or religious influences that can impact the Enneagram energy. Still, these factors do not fundamentally change a person's dominant Enneagram type.

- No one can tell you where you stand on the Enneagram map. You find your place by reading about and exploring all aspects of the nine types. Tests can help you narrow down the choices, and you may find your type by process of elimination. Tests are not always the defining factor of where you stand on the Enneagram map; the tests' quality matters.

KEY DESCRIPTORS OF
THE NINE TYPES

The descriptors for each Enneagram type listed below begin on the high side of the energy and transition into the low side of the energy.

THE BODY CENTER

8 self-confident, authoritative, hardworking, strong-willed, forceful, passionate, outspoken, independent, protective, abundant energy, maintaining power and control, defensive, combative, "invulnerable," harsh, rageful, vengeful, boastful, demonstrative, tyrannical, omnipotent

9 receptive, reassuring, agreeable, considerate, quiet, easygoing, thoughtful, accepting, supportive, accommodating, dependable, stable, hardworking, pragmatic, complacent, disengaged, emotionally indolent, indifferent, angry, stubborn, dissociated, numb, apathetic

1 principled, purposeful, organized, ethical, fastidious, fair, objective, sense of mission, practical action, high standards, inner critic, highly critical, impatient, repressed, angry, controlling, perfectionistic, puritanical, resentful, emotionally constricted, scolding, abrasive, punitive, inflexible

THE HEART CENTER

2 generous, empathetic, helpful, thoughtful, caring, reliable, compassionate, kind, overly considerate, people-pleasing, seductive, intrusive, possessive, seeking validation, angry, resentful, hurt, manipulative, flattering, demonstrative, low self-esteem/value

3 hardworking, dedicated, driven, ambitious, resourceful, impressive, motivated, highly skilled, distinguished, pragmatic, opportunistic, calculating, narcissistic, impostor syndrome, seeking validation and attention, social climber, arrogant, unprincipled, self-centered, conceited

4 emotional, empathetic, creative, unique, connected, deep, romantic, authentic, eccentric, poetic, introspective, sensitive, moody, manipulative, judgmental, self-conscious, tormented, dark, depressive, angry, lost, self-destructive, hopeless, despair, macabre, self-absorbed

THE HEAD CENTER

5 competent, capable, cerebral, wise, highly skilled, well-rounded, eccentric, pioneering, complex, perceptive, independent, inventive, visionary, secretive, withdrawn, antagonistic, cynical, argumentative, reclusive, intellectually arrogant, self-destructive, nihilistic, erratic

6 innovative, structured, hardworking, intensely loyal, reliable, security-oriented, troubleshooting, revolutionary, engaging, contradictory, dependent, indecisive, untrusting, defensive, reactive, fearful, insecure, stubborn, suspicious, erratic, worst-case scenario, panicked, paranoid

7 free-spirited, fun, happy, curious, joyful, optimistic, adventurous, fast learners, well-rounded, humorous, bold, vivacious, life of the party, flaky, self-centered, narcissistic, emotionally stunted, insensitive, impulsive, escapist mentality, erratic, compulsive, panic-stricken, avoidance, jaded

Which descriptors from your Enneagram energy
do you resonate with the most and why?

_____

_____

_____

_____

_____

_____

_____

_____

_____

_____

_____

_____

_____

Enneagram Type Six

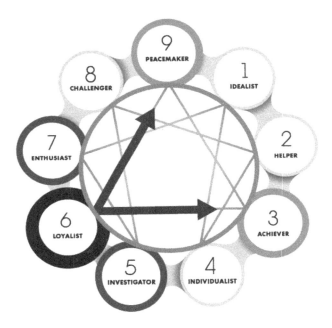

DESCRIPTORS FOR SIX ENERGY

loyal, prepared, security-oriented, self-sacrificing,
committed, reliable, hardworking, responsible,
trustworthy, innovative, cooperative, cautious, anxious,
worst-case scenario, defiant, reactive, self-doubt,
distrust, fearful, scattered, panicked, indecisive, evasive

Basic Desire: to have security and stability, to have support and guidance

Basic Fear: to feel unstable or without guidance, to be without support

Core Motivation: to have security and backup plans, to feel supported by others, to have certitude and reassurance, to test the attitudes of others toward you, to fight against anxiety and insecurity

Passion/The Personal Challenge: Fear—uncertainty and a deep distrust in all things: self, people, information, systems, authority, actions, beliefs, and behaviors

Fixation/The Trap: Cowardice—a paralyzing pattern of panic, distrust, inaction, and helplessness when faced with challenges to stability and security

Virtue/The Gift: Courage—an acceptance of trust in self and others allows for purpose and strength in all things

Wings: Five and Seven

Arrows: Nine and Three

Sixes want to be:

- safe and secure

- supported by others

- in a position of certitude and reassurance

- able to test the attitudes and feelings of others

- able to fight against anxiety and insecurity

- in a position of predictability as a way of defending self

Sixes do not want to be:

- abandoned or left without guidance and support

- in a position of uncertainty

- forced to deal with contradictory expectations

- pressured or forced to accept new ideas rapidly

- in a position to have belief systems and trusted sources of stability questioned

LEVELS OF DEVELOPMENT
AS A TYPE SIX

Healthy Levels of Development

When operating within the healthy Levels of Development, you can honor the value in truth and duty and stand up to destructive forces. You may challenge the systems designed to create disparities and inequities, all while managing the polarity of fear and integrity. Your courageous spirit and the true force of your inner strength begin to guide you on your journey of becoming a leader in the fight for collective security. The anxiety and fear that once paralyzed you now evolve and make space for a decisive and truth-seeking champion who recognizes your fear as a wake-up call to take action. You will stand up and fight against any challenge to the stability and security of any human or group, cutting through the false narratives and the negativity with courage and compassion.

Average Levels of Development

Most humans reside within these average levels and fluctuate up or down depending on the circumstances they find themselves in. As a Six drops down into the average Levels of Development, the ego agenda begins to take over. The fluctuations can create opportunities for you to pause and cultivate the presence needed to examine your thoughts and actions and course correct. This allows you to move up in the levels and avoid falling back into unhealthy patterns of behavior and thought. However, as the ability for self-reflection and course correction wanes, you can become suspicious of others and your own beliefs. You become reactive and unpredictable, focusing on the threats to your own security. You become fearful of change, and your struggle to course correct is caused by ambiguity. You can become fearful and apathetic and struggle to acknowledge opportunities for hope or humanity. You may turn critical, panicky, passive-aggressive and sarcastic. In the average levels, you are likely a wounded individual attempting to conceal your true fears by lashing out with distrustful and irrational beliefs and negativity aimed at anyone who threatens your perception of stability and security. Despite having the innate ability to see the big picture and access all perspectives in question, you often choose to select whatever data supports you in your quest to justify your own fear. Trust becomes a primary challenge as you drop lower into the Levels of Development. The fear and anxiety at these levels can morph into a combination of uncertainty and distrust and cause you to drop further down the levels. It takes a great deal of self-reflection and inner work to rise through the levels and avoid dropping further.

Unhealthy Levels of Development

As you drop into the unhealthy levels, you can become incredibly unstable, nihilistic, irrationally belligerent, and self-destructive. You begin to justify your actions and beliefs from the unhealthy energy of Type Six. Fear, distrust, and paranoia are the primary motivators that distort your reality, resulting in disdain for humans who may be perceived as a threat or challenge to your way of life. As an unhealthy Six, you are likely to hold on to an unquestioned loyalty in favor of unfair and biased systems already in place out of fear of being left on uncertain or shaky ground. As you drop lower and lower into the levels, you become deeply distrustful of others but also of yourself; you are stuck in a destructive pattern of indecision and suspicion. Fearful, unstable, delusional, and unquestioningly loyal, you may cause deeper divides between your authentic self and other people. You become irrational and are prone to outbursts of truly detestable behaviors toward other people. You may have lost control of your inner narrative and allowed your fears to pour out through biased, bigoted, and deeply destructive remarks.

You can refer back to the Levels of Development to see where you are at any point in time. Make notes on your progress below:

_____

_____

_____

_____

_____

_____

_____

WINGS

Remember, you have access to both wings. Some people identify strongly with one wing energy over the other, but both wings still affect how your dominant type appears.

SIX WITH A STRONG FIVE WING

Practical problem-solving, passion for finding truth and fighting unfair systems, pessimistic and cynical, emotionally stunted, detached, cold and aloof, socially awkward and insensitive

SIX WITH A STRONG SEVEN WING

Dedicated to a cause, deeply connected to the well-being of others, loyal and sociable, optimistic and engaged, doubt in all things, selfish, indecisive and scattered, focused on negative, insensitive comments

ARROWS

Remember, you have access to both arrows, and you can move freely between these connections. This movement allows you to pick up positive and negative energies as needed and creates a warning system and a path for growth.

SIX'S ARROW TO THREE

Confidence and trust in self creates decisive action and courage, outgoing and assertive, narrow focus creates an isolated perspective, self-centered behaviors to gain leverage or security, overwhelm and exhaustion

SIX'S ARROW TO NINE

Balanced perspective and a drive to find collective peace and harmony through courageous action, a calm and focused approach to decision-making, maintain the status quo, disregard for others, detached and apathetic

INSTINCTS

As balanced human beings, we naturally have all three instincts within us. However, we have a dominant instinct that we feel most comfortable with and a secondary instinct to support the dominant one. The third instinct is usually the least developed, therefore, an area that manifests as an unseen personal challenge.

SELF-PRESERVATION SIX

As a Self-Preservation Six, you are more focused on building security and stability through mutual responsibility and reciprocal partnerships. You do not hide your fears from others and often will utilize your insecurity to gain support and guidance. You rely on creating dependencies and making sure you have backup plans for when things will inevitably go wrong, even when everything is going right. You have probably made peace with anxiety and worry controlling your life, but you also can experience moments of courage when you step out of the anxiety and allow for trust to manifest.

SOCIAL SIX

As a Social Six, you tend to be slightly more extroverted than the other instincts as you enjoy making connections and sharing your warmth and generosity with others. While you are more socially motivated, you also need space to process your fears around security and support. You can have a hard time working on developing your own identity or growing as an individual. Instead of finding what works for you personally, you tend to rely on group consensus and allow others to influence your beliefs and behaviors.

SEXUAL SIX

As a Sexual Six, you focus your energy on finding ways to make yourself appear strong and in control like Eights; or like Fours, who can actively seek out a rescuer, you will find people who will provide security and support. You can use this outward display of strength, power, and control either personally or by proxy, to calm your fears and anxiety around being left without guidance or support. You tend to test others in the hopes of confirming your own security and stability. As a Sexual Six, you carry the most doubt and distrust both of yourself and of others, as you are constantly trying to calm your anxiety by challenging your situations and the people you care about.

SIX'S RESPONSES
TO CONFLICTS

UNHEALTHY REACTION

Distrust, avoidance, external blame, irrational defensiveness, cowardice, inflexibility, passive-aggressive behavior, ambivalence, highly reactive and defensive, dividing others into groups, irrational outbursts of panicked paranoia, radical response to "outsiders," fanaticism, violent outbursts in extreme cases, defending your way of thinking in order to dismiss or demean anything that may challenge your stability, making insensitive comments, lacking in empathy and genuine human emotion

HEALTHY REACTION

Truth-seeking, challenging of status quo or destructive leadership, sacrifice, courage, speaking out against threats to collective security and safety, standing up and finding solutions when witnessing unfair practices harming other people, remaining loyal to your beliefs when acting from a kindhearted and courageous space, recognizing your fear as a wake-up call to take action, you are no longer paralyzed by your anxiety, fighting against any challenge to the stability and security of any human or group, cutting through the false narratives and the negativity with courage and compassion

Reflections on your experience of unhealthy and healthy responses:

_____

_____

_____

_____

_____

_____

_____

EXAMPLES OF SIX ENERGY

Tom Hanks, Bono, Prince Harry, Richard Nixon, Sigmund Freud, Robert F. Kennedy, Malcolm X, George H. W. Bush, J. R. R. Tolkien, Michael Moore, Jimmy Kimmel, Spike Lee, J. Edgar Hoover, Mindy Kaling, Rush Limbaugh, Ellen DeGeneres, Lewis Black, Chris Rock, Larry David, Mel Gibson, John Grisham, Mike Tyson, Bruce Springsteen

Explore your connection to one or more of these people who demonstrate strong Six energy. What is it about their character or personality that reminds you most of yourself?

_____

_____

_____

_____

_____

_____

_____

_____

_____

_____

_____

_____

_____

_____

_____

_____

_____

How do you experience the different elements
of Six energy within yourself?

_____

_____

_____

_____

_____

_____

_____

_____

_____

_____

_____

_____

_____

_____

_____

_____

_____

_____

_____

_____

_____

What is your experience like with other people who exhibit Six energy?

Reflections on
BEING AN
ENNEAGRAM SIX

As you embark on this profound inner journey, it's essential to take a moment to revisit the very origin of your path. Within this section, we invite you to reflect upon the beginnings of your Enneagram journey and how it gently unfolded before you. Delving into past feelings and behaviors is a natural and important aspect of this process.

As a Type Six, your greatest strength lies in your remarkable capacity to be thoroughly prepared for anything that the Universe might send your way. The following prompts are designed to offer you a chance for deep reflection, guiding you on a journey of self-discovery and personal growth.

It's quite likely that you had specific reactions when you first discovered your dominant energy at Type Six. These reactions are all part of the ongoing journey as you gradually transition from mere reactions to intentional responses. It's essential to explore your feelings but not to become ensnared or overwhelmed by what you feel. Remember, feelings are transient by nature. As you navigate through your emotions, you'll discover immense fulfillment at the deeper layers of this exploration. Embrace your innate curiosity and approach this journey with the wonder of a beginner's mind as you unveil more and more about your authentic self and how you present yourself to the world. In connecting with the reality of your inner guidance and greatness, you may be pleasantly surprised by the fears that once held you back.

It's important to recognize that not every attribute, characteristic, or behavior associated with Type Six may fully align with your unique experience of your energy. This presents a rich opportunity to unearth aspects of your being that have previously eluded your awareness. The discovery of your authentic self will not only open your mind but also mend your heart, and rejuvenate your body in profound ways. This deep dive allows your spirit to embrace and embody your core values in perfect harmony with your natural gift of being able to move into action as you have already hoped for the best but prepared for the worst. We wholeheartedly encourage you not to hold back but to embrace this journey as it carries you to uncharted territories within your own being, revealing facets of yourself you have yet to explore. This is our heartfelt wish for you.

Grounding Meditation

As I move into self-reflection and internal exploration,
I will meditate on these prompts and gently notice
what comes up as I breathe into stillness.

I am ready to begin with three cleansing breaths.

I am releasing any tension that I am holding
in my body with each exhale.

I am grounded and present to the sensations in my body.

I am open and aware of the feelings in my heart.

I am not attached to the thoughts that float by.

I am ready to explore what being a Six means to me.

I will embrace all aspects of my personality and gently
work toward becoming more accepting of myself.

My reactions when I discovered my dominant energy as a Type Six:

_____

_____

_____

_____

_____

_____

_____

_____

_____

_____

_____

_____

_____

_____

_____

_____

_____

_____

_____

_____

_____

_____

_____

My feelings about being a Six:

_____

_____

_____

_____

_____

_____

_____

_____

_____

_____

_____

_____

_____

_____

_____

_____

_____

_____

_____

_____

_____

_____

_____

My hopes for discovering more about my Six energy:

My fears around seeing myself as I truly am:

_____

_____

_____

_____

_____

_____

_____

_____

_____

_____

_____

_____

_____

_____

_____

_____

_____

_____

_____

_____

_____

Observations about myself that support Six as my dominant type:

_____
_____
_____
_____
_____
_____
_____
_____
_____
_____
_____
_____
_____
_____
_____
_____
_____
_____
_____
_____
_____
_____
_____

Aspects and descriptors of Six energy that I do not feel connected with:

_____

_____

_____

_____

_____

_____

_____

_____

_____

_____

_____

Are these aspects I do not feel connected with indicators
of any personal challenges that I may overlook?

_____

_____

_____

_____

_____

_____

_____

_____

_____

_____

What are my core values that align with my Six energy?

Reflections on my actions and beliefs around my core values:

Ways I have honored my core values recently:

_____

_____

_____

_____

_____

_____

_____

_____

_____

_____

_____

_____

_____

_____

_____

_____

_____

_____

_____

_____

_____

_____

_____

What do I wish people knew about me?

_____

_____

_____

_____

_____

_____

_____

_____

_____

_____

_____

_____

_____

_____

_____

_____

_____

_____

_____

_____

_____

_____

Reflections on
MY EARLY MESSAGES
AND EXPERIENCES

As you embark on this journey, take a moment to reflect on the early messages and messengers that have shaped your path. You might discover that your childhood experiences with the powerful energy of Type Six instilled in you a profound need for guidance and stability.

These initial reactions and responses, etched deep within you, were not merely fleeting notions but lasting imprints. These reactions and responses, woven into the tapestry of your being, were absorbed with an innocence you couldn't fully grasp at the time. They were not mere words passing through one ear and out the other; rather, they etched themselves into your soul, sometimes hidden away for years, waiting for the profound inner work that now beckons you.

As you transitioned into adulthood, these feelings became an integral part of your approach to life. They gave rise to an internal narrative that emphasized seeking solutions, stability, and guidance while harboring doubt in your own judgment. This narrative was your complex way of managing the anxiety and fear, but it was also the catalyst for many of your challenges.

Reflecting on your past experiences, you may recognize behaviors and tendencies closely aligned with the energy at Type Six. As you reflect on your life's unfolding, who or what stands out as a pivotal influence in your development? Comparing and contrasting your life experiences, the individuals who left lasting imprints, and the indelible impressions etched in your heart is an integral part of this introspective expedition.

Embrace your identity as an Enneagram Six, not dwelling upon the shadows but rather celebrating the rays of positivity that have helped mold you into the remarkable person you've become. Navigating from Six to the brighter, more optimistic energies of the Enneagram may seem challenging, but there exists a profound connection to joy, togetherness, and love as you delve into the depths of your past. Exploring the upsides and downsides of your childhood can help illuminate that path. Consider the moments of childhood joy and happiness; these memories provide a direct route to unlocking your authentic self.

Grounding Meditation

As I move into self-reflection and internal exploration,
I will meditate on these prompts and gently notice
what comes up as I breathe into stillness.

I am ready to begin with three cleansing breaths.

I am inhaling peace and exhaling tension.

I am ready to embark on a journey into my past.

I will honor my experience as I recall childhood memories.

My past does not define me.

I can explore what was, accept what is, and embrace what will be.

My most vivid memory of how my Six energy
showed up when I was a child:

_____

_____

_____

_____

_____

_____

_____

_____

_____

_____

_____

_____

_____

_____

_____

_____

_____

_____

_____

_____

_____

_____

_____

These are the people and experiences that brought me the most felt sense of guidance and stability during my childhood:

_____

_____

_____

_____

_____

_____

_____

_____

_____

_____

_____

_____

_____

_____

_____

_____

_____

_____

_____

_____

_____

_____

I can create space in my life for more of these positive influences by:

_____

_____

_____

_____

_____

_____

_____

_____

_____

_____

_____

_____

_____

_____

_____

_____

_____

_____

_____

_____

_____

_____

What plans, goals, and hopes for my future did I have as a child?

Activities I enjoyed as a child:

Reflections on how these activities brought
feelings of pure joy and happiness:

_____

_____

_____

_____

_____

_____

_____

_____

_____

_____

_____

_____

_____

_____

_____

_____

_____

_____

_____

_____

_____

_____

_____

Happiness is part
of the flow of life.

If you remain rigid,
then happiness will
flow right past you.

Allow yourself
the gift of letting
go and ease into the
flow of whatever may
come your way.

I can cultivate small moments of happiness in my everyday life by:

Reflections on

MY PURPOSE AND
MY "PUZZLE PIECE"

Let's imagine the world as a puzzle, and envision each one of us holding a piece that, when placed, helps create a more complete and harmonious world. You possess a truly unique gift to offer to the world; imagine it as if you are the holder of a vital piece of a grand, intricate puzzle. Yet to truly offer this gift, we must be willing to embark on our own inner journey.

When we embrace this inner work, we gain the strength and clarity needed to step forward and make our unique contribution. This courageous act sets a beautiful chain reaction in motion, allowing others to find the inspiration and courage to contribute as well.

In the upcoming section, we extend a warm invitation to you, encouraging you to (re)awaken the passions and interests that stir deep within your soul, those beautiful aspects of yourself that you'd love to revive and share with the world. You might notice a strong emotional response to social injustices; this very reaction could be a hidden passion or a point of personal growth waiting to be unveiled. Your dedication to a particular societal issue could hold the key to discovering your unique place and voice in contributing to the collective healing of humanity. Perhaps your heart resonates deeply with environmental causes, or you're deeply affected by the suffering of animals. This is your precious opportunity to unearth and delve into what truly matters to you.

Consider what consistently draws your attention and captivates your mind—whether it's art, music, literature, social causes, theater, science, spirituality, parenting, or family. Why do these topics continue to surface for you? Use this opportunity to delve deeper into the aspects of your life where you find an abundance of energy or even areas that may initially appear exhausting. This is your chance to sculpt and refine your unique puzzle piece (and yes, we all have one or more) so that you can stand with gratitude and presence, fully aware of the significance of your contribution. As we awaken to our own purpose, we naturally have the capacity to awaken those around us, igniting a chain reaction of positive change.

Explore the boundless possibilities that lie ahead, and remember that your piece of the puzzle is invaluable to creating a world that's more complete, compassionate, and connected.

Grounding Meditation

As I move into self-reflection and internal exploration,
I will meditate on these prompts and gently notice
what comes up as I breathe into stillness.

I am ready to begin with three cleansing breaths.

I am releasing any tension that I am holding
in my body with each exhale.

I am inhaling into the wholeness of the Universe
and exhaling whatever may be troubling me.

I am open to exploring my place in the world.

I am willing to explore my purpose and (re)discover the
unique puzzle piece I hold to contribute to the world.

My life has meaning, and my presence matters.

I am accepting of whatever comes up for me at this moment.

What contributions do I want to make in this world?

Reflections on how I align my daily actions with
my deeper sense of finding the truth:

What inspires me?

_____

_____

_____

_____

_____

_____

_____

_____

_____

_____

_____

_____

_____

_____

_____

_____

_____

_____

_____

_____

_____

_____

_____

How have I limited myself in finding sources of inspiration? How can I open myself to new experiences? Have I considered engaging with new people, places, music, art, literature, and so on?

I am very passionate about:

_____

_____

_____

_____

_____

_____

_____

_____

_____

_____

_____

_____

_____

_____

_____

_____

_____

_____

_____

_____

_____

_____

What comes up for me when I think about the activities,
relationships, and causes that I am drawn to?

_____

_____

_____

_____

_____

_____

_____

_____

_____

_____

_____

_____

_____

_____

_____

_____

_____

_____

_____

_____

The quality
of your life
will reflect
how deep you
are willing
to go to touch
your own soul.

What personal, professional, spiritual, and/or life
roles contribute to my sense of identity?

_____

_____

_____

_____

_____

_____

_____

_____

_____

_____

_____

_____

_____

_____

_____

_____

_____

_____

_____

_____

_____

_____

What areas of my life make me feel connected
to something bigger than myself?

_____

_____

_____

_____

_____

_____

_____

_____

_____

_____

_____

_____

_____

_____

_____

_____

_____

_____

_____

_____

What gets in the way of being able to participate in the things that make me feel connected to something bigger than myself?

Reflections on my current projects, work, and/or endeavors:

How are these feeding my spirit or draining my energy?

Reflections on
HOW MY SIX
ENERGY SHOWS UP

As someone who finds their place as a Type Six on the Enneagram, it can be illuminating to delve into how your inner narrative and the yearning for stability and security influence your energy. When your sense of security is firm, you often carry yourself with a sense of justification in your actions and a comfort in your behaviors. Yet a subtle lack of trust lingers, manifesting as an inclination to entertain worst-case scenarios.

This tendency becomes particularly noticeable in situations where change, minimal planning, and safety are of utmost importance. It's in these moments that your unwavering nature can take a step back, giving way to a default state of fear and the expectation of impending disaster. This shift can lead to distorted desires for finding guidance and perpetuate a cycle of anxiety, often accompanied by extreme actions.

It's at this juncture that the path of inner work beckons you, offering the opportunity to raise the vibration of your energy to a healthier level and realign with your inner wisdom. As you shed the burden of fear and the inclination to catastrophize, you find yourself beautifully attuned to your spirit.

In this newfound alignment, love, trust, and an authentic capacity to stand beside and serve humanity begin to flourish within you. The tight grip that fear and anxiety used to have on your life begins to ease, and you embrace life's flow as a precious gift. With this trust in the unseen currents of benevolence, your presence becomes a beacon, openly received by others, and the impact you make in the world is not just acknowledged but cherished and welcomed by all fortunate enough to encounter you.

Grounding Meditation

As I move into self-reflection and internal exploration,
I will meditate on these prompts and gently notice
what comes up as I breathe into stillness.

I am ready to begin with three cleansing breaths.

I am releasing any tension that I am holding
in my body with each exhale.

I am inhaling into presence and exhaling anxiety.

I am ready to explore my Sixness.

I will allow myself to reflect on how I show up to myself and others.

I will acknowledge any anxiety and worry that arises
with Grace and compassion for myself.

I will embrace all parts of my being as valid and valuable.

I will release the need to overthink things and honor
what comes up for me in the moment.

Reflect back on the "Levels of Development" section (page 14) for this exercise.

I was aware of the high side of my Six energy this week when:

_____

_____

_____

_____

_____

_____

_____

_____

_____

_____

_____

_____

_____

_____

_____

_____

_____

_____

_____

_____

Reflect back on the "Levels of Development" section (page 14) for this exercise.

I was aware of the low side of my Six energy this week when:

_____

_____

_____

_____

_____

_____

_____

_____

_____

_____

_____

_____

_____

_____

_____

_____

_____

_____

_____

_____

Fear is a mechanism of survival that demands a delicate balance; using it as a motivating force, yet avoiding being trapped and controlled by its formidable power.

My reflections on what fear means to me:

_____

_____

_____

_____

_____

_____

_____

_____

_____

_____

_____

_____

_____

_____

_____

_____

_____

_____

_____

_____

_____

_____

_____

_____

_____

_____

_____

_____

_____

My reactions to feeling unsafe and unsure:

_____
_____
_____
_____
_____
_____
_____
_____
_____
_____
_____
_____
_____
_____
_____
_____
_____
_____
_____
_____
_____
_____
_____

What parts of myself do I hide from others and why?

Ways that I experience challenges to my belief systems:

_____

_____

_____

_____

_____

_____

_____

_____

_____

_____

_____

_____

_____

_____

_____

_____

_____

_____

_____

_____

_____

_____

_____

_____

How do I express love and affection?

When do I feel prepared and unafraid?

My reflections on how I make decisions:

_____

_____

_____

_____

_____

_____

_____

_____

_____

_____

_____

_____

_____

_____

_____

_____

_____

_____

_____

_____

_____

_____

_____

You must embrace
your own being
and accept yourself
exactly as you are.
This is a first
step in belonging.
Never let anyone
determine whether
or not you belong.

That choice is yours.

What does belonging mean to me? How have I sought
out belonging and connection in my life?

What do other people do for me that makes me feel seen?

How do I make others feel seen?

How do other people describe me?

Fill the page with words, phrases, and drawings.
Allow for the flow of creativity and freedom.

How do I describe myself?

Fill the page with words, phrases, and drawings.
Allow for the flow of creativity and freedom.

Reflections on
TRUST

As a Type Six, you may be all too familiar with intricate interplay of trust and fear. You've likely found yourself, time and again, unraveling the threads of possibilities, weighing the benefits and risks with each decision, whether they be grand or minute. It's your way of navigating the tapestry of daily life, but at times, this very pattern can become paralyzing.

The need for security in every aspect of your existence stems from the looming shadow of fear and anxiety that's closely tied to self-doubt and trust. Doubt about your ability to stand and move forward without external guidance and trust, both in others and yourself, can be a daunting challenge.

In your journey, you may have found yourself amid situations where decision-making seems elusive because there appears to be no beacon of trustworthiness to guide you. Your internal narrative may have unintentionally kept you from forming meaningful connections with others and deprived you of the beautiful gift of trust, which holds the key to genuine stability and guidance.

The true voyage begins when you unearth the capacity to trust yourself. In doing so, you'll realize that the wellspring of wisdom you seek lies within, removing the need to look elsewhere. Learning to trust and gracefully accept the outcomes of circumstances beyond your control becomes a constant companion on your path to a rich and satisfying life. In the face of challenging decisions, you might have noticed the inner committee playing out scenarios in your mind. Pay attention to when this tends to stall the momentum of the action that needs to be taken. Reflecting on your past experiences can offer a fresh perspective on your actions and behaviors, guiding you toward trusting your own inner compass. Remember that to trust others, you must first embrace trust in yourself.

Trust and forgiveness, intertwined companions in the human experience, form a complex concept often misunderstood. Beyond benefiting others, forgiveness frees you from emotional burdens, opening the path to love and happiness. It enables your authentic expression of love, aligning with your creation. Great ascended masters stress the importance of forgiveness, providing invaluable lessons we sometimes forget. Remember, forgiveness is integral to self-love, allowing your authentic self to return to innocence and purity by freeing yourself from pain. It's the ultimate act of self-respect, empowering and embracing your inner strength.

Grounding Meditation

As I move into self-reflection and internal exploration,
I will meditate on these prompts and gently notice
what comes up as I breathe into stillness.

I am ready to begin with three cleansing breaths.

I am inhaling into presence and positivity and
exhaling cynicism and negativity.

I can acknowledge my complicated relationship with trust.

I am willing to take a leap of faith when I need to.

I will access the courage and focus I need to
begin to cultivate more trust in my life.

I will remain in presence and choose a path
of empathy and compassion.

What/who do I trust and why?

_____

_____

_____

_____

_____

_____

_____

_____

_____

_____

What/who do I distrust and why?

_____

_____

_____

_____

_____

_____

_____

_____

_____

_____

_____

How do my challenges around trust affect how I view and treat others?

What does it look like when I allow myself to trust my inner judgments?

What does it look like when someone breaks my trust?

Can I allow myself to trust someone fully and accept
the outcome? How can I explore this further?

What steps can I take to pause and determine my course of action when the committee in my head has taken over?

_____

_____

_____

_____

_____

_____

_____

_____

_____

_____

_____

_____

_____

_____

_____

_____

_____

_____

_____

_____

_____

Reflecting back on how I may have been unsure of myself and suspicious of others, how could I have handled certain situations differently?

_____

_____

_____

_____

_____

_____

_____

_____

_____

_____

_____

_____

_____

_____

_____

_____

_____

_____

_____

_____

_____

_____

What am I willing to let go of in order to allow myself to begin
to trust people who I have deemed untrustworthy?

_____

_____

_____

_____

_____

_____

_____

_____

_____

_____

_____

_____

_____

_____

_____

_____

_____

_____

_____

_____

What/who do I need to forgive?

_____
_____
_____
_____
_____
_____
_____
_____
_____
_____
_____
_____
_____
_____
_____
_____
_____
_____
_____

Forgiveness doesn't excuse their behavior. Forgiveness prevents their behavior from destroying your heart.

UNKNOWN

Do I know how to forgive? What is holding me back from
accessing forgiveness for myself and others?

_____

_____

_____

_____

_____

_____

_____

_____

_____

_____

_____

_____

_____

_____

_____

_____

_____

_____

_____

_____

_____

We are surrounded by Grace in every moment of our lives. Grace always comes through when we allow ourselves to embrace and experience the warmth of its existence.

Let love and light in.

Allow Grace to lead your actions today.

What does Grace look like for me as a Six?

Reflections on
MY RELATIONSHIP TO ANXIETY AND FEAR

As a Six, you might encounter a formidable wall of fear and anxiety, one that may guard an unhealed or unexplored internal wound. This wall can act as a barrier, preventing you from accessing your authentic self, and how you address or ignore it can vary from person to person. For some, this fear might originate from early memories of feeling insecure, unsafe, overwhelmed, unsupported, unfulfilled, or alone. Each individual copes with their fear uniquely, but when we find ourselves trapped in unhealthy patterns of behavior and belief, this internal fear can often manifest outwardly, aimed at deflecting our own fears onto others in some way or another.

As someone who resonates with Type Six, you've woven a complex tapestry of anxiety, fear, and courage into your life. It's likely that your mind has become a bustling committee, constantly vigilant for potential threats and diligently crafting backup plans for every scenario. Seeking solutions and assessing potential risks to your safety, stability, and security is your method of soothing your fears and anxieties. The future holds your attention, and you are resolute in your determination to ward off anything or anyone that may jeopardize your plans for establishing a stable foundation. Behind many of your actions lies a profound well of insecurity and hesitancy, often stemming from a lack of self-confidence and apprehension about trusting not only yourself but also others.

In this next section, you are invited to gently explore the roots of your fear and anxiety and begin to address these emotions in a healthy and productive manner. As you engage in these self-reflective exercises, remember to be kind and compassionate toward yourself. Whatever arises, whether it's a surge of emotion or a long-forgotten memory, treat it with the tenderness it deserves. These exercises are thoughtfully designed to guide you through the challenges of your energy, allowing you to reconnect with the inherent goodness, love, and light that reside within you. Embrace this path of self-discovery, and you'll find that it leads to profound personal growth and a deeper connection with your authentic self.

Grounding Meditation

As I move into self-reflection and internal exploration,
I will meditate on these prompts and gently notice
what comes up as I breathe into stillness.

I am ready to begin with three cleansing breaths.

I am inhaling a sense of calm and peace and
exhaling tension and anxiety.

I acknowledge my fear and anxiety, and I am willing
to gently explore what's underneath.

I will explore my relationship to my fear
with perseverance and courage.

I will explore my relationship to my anxiety
with patience and understanding.

I accept fear and anxiety as natural human emotions.

My fear does not define who I am.

My anxiety cannot control me.

I will accept my fear and anxiety as an internal warning system
to seek out opportunities for growth and self-reflection.

What/who makes me anxious or fearful?

What is the difference between these two emotions,
and what does it look like for me personally?

_____

_____

_____

_____

_____

_____

_____

_____

_____

_____

_____

_____

_____

_____

_____

_____

_____

_____

_____

_____

_____

How do I express my anxiety and fear? What does it look like?

How is my capacity for trust tied to my fears and anxiety?

I notice I tend to create worst-case scenarios in my decision-making when:

_____

_____

_____

_____

_____

_____

_____

_____

_____

_____

_____

_____

_____

_____

_____

_____

_____

_____

_____

_____

_____

_____

_____

As a Six, I have probably experienced "amnesia of my success."
What have I successfully accomplished that I
have not given myself credit for?

_____

_____

_____

_____

_____

_____

_____

_____

_____

_____

_____

_____

_____

_____

_____

_____

_____

_____

_____

Reflections on a time I made a decision in the
moment and it worked out for the best:

_____

_____

_____

_____

_____

_____

_____

_____

_____

_____

_____

_____

_____

_____

_____

_____

_____

_____

_____

_____

_____

_____

What does it look like when my fear and anxiety take over?

_____

_____

_____

_____

_____

_____

_____

_____

_____

What are a few small actions I can take when I
begin to sense my anxiety taking over?

_____

_____

_____

_____

_____

_____

_____

_____

_____

Reflections on
MY VIRTUE OF
COURAGE

The virtue for you as a Type Six is courage. This gift empowers you to wholeheartedly embrace the natural ebb and flow of life. As you let your inner strength be your guiding light, a remarkable transformation takes place. The anxious exterior that often conceals your true essence gives way to a grounded, trustworthy, and confident self.

When you're able to step into your virtue, you cultivate the courage to stand up against destructive forces and challenge the systems that perpetuate disparities and inequities. All the while you navigate the delicate balance between fear and integrity. Your courageous spirit, fueled by the authentic force of your inner strength, propels you on a journey toward becoming a leader in the collective quest for security. Courage emerges when you intentionally and wholeheartedly commit to the inner work, moving closer to the gifts that reside on the higher side of Six.

On this path toward your virtue, familiar obstacles may appear, particularly the trap of cowardice, the fixation for an Enneagram Six. The profound fear of losing guidance, support, and stability can trap you within your thoughts, leaving you paralyzed by anxiety and fear, unable to take that crucial step forward. This protective stance, while well-intentioned, can keep you confined within the boundaries of your comfort zone, resistant to new ideas and hesitant to trust those who challenge the familiar.

This is where the transformative inner work comes into play. As you address the roadblocks along your path, you'll begin to foster a newfound trust, both in yourself and in the world around you. The fear and anxiety that once held you captive evolve into a catalyst for decisive action, for seeking truth and championing your beliefs.

This invitation to embrace transformation ushers in a phase of self-discovery, where you reclaim your inner strength and courage, emerging as a resolute leader and truth-seeker. Here is where you can fully embrace your virtue of courage, finding a harmonious balance and renewed trust in the world that surrounds you. Exploring the path to this virtue is yet another step on your journey to unearth your authentic self.

As you navigate this section, try to remain present and open-minded. Rediscover the resilience of your inner guidance through trust and courage, and embrace the profound power that lies within you.

Grounding Meditation

As I move into self-reflection and internal exploration,
I will meditate on each of these prompts and gently notice
what comes up for me as I breathe into stillness.

I am ready to begin with three cleansing breaths.

I am releasing any tension that I am holding
in my body with each exhale.

I am allowing myself the gift of peace and
courage as I begin this exploration.

As I explore courage, I seek out opportunities
to allow it to flow naturally.

Courage is my access to Grace.

Courage is always present within me.

I allow myself to embrace the gift of courage by
releasing what no longer serves me.

How has courage manifested in my life, and what did it bring?

How has courage eluded me?
What comes up for me by asking this question?

Courage
moves us away
from fear and
lights our path
to conquer
the darkness.

What am I willing to surrender to embrace courage?

Reflecting on my relationship with trust, indecision, anxiety, and fear, can I explore what my path to the embodiment of courage looks like?

When do I notice my fear and anxiety fading and my
ability to access the virtue of courage developing?

What am I willing to sacrifice to step into a courageous space?
Can I give specific examples?

What are a few mantras I will use daily to bring myself back to the present and move into a space where I can access the virtue of equanimity?

Example: I am able to trust my inner judgment and move forward with courage and intentional presence.

Discovering Connections to
OTHER ENNEAGRAM ENERGIES

Consider the Enneagram energies as nine individual gifts, each uniquely enriching the tapestry of your being. Within each of us, these nine energies coexist, and far too often, our fixation on our Enneagram type limits our perspective, hindering exploration of the eight other invaluable energies residing within us. It's vital to recognize that every human being requires the presence of these nine energies to achieve wholeness and completeness.

At each point of the Enneagram, a precious gift awaits, illuminating the path of self-discovery. At point One the gift is integrity, a beacon that guides you with a resolute moral compass. Point Two bestows the gift of pure love, fostering a spirit of generosity and an open heart for giving and receiving. Point Three endows you with the drive to accomplish and achieve great things, not just for personal gain but for the greater good of all. Point Four graces you with the capacity to embrace the world's beauty, holding it through love, empathy, and profound compassion while connecting deeply with human emotions. Point Five gifts you with the power of observation and the ability to discern solutions that might otherwise go unnoticed. At point Six you receive the gift of resilience, enabling you to cultivate the awareness of what is needed to keep us all protected, prepared, and unwavering in the face of adversity. Point Seven brings the gift of optimism, positivity, and spontaneity, infusing even the most challenging tasks with the spirit of joyfulness. Point Eight's gift is leadership, guiding us forward with the purity and strength of an innocent heart, always mindful of keeping our collective well-being intact. Finally, at point Nine, you are blessed with the gift of pure peace, a peace that transcends understanding and can only arise from a heart transformed by light and love.

Imagine that someone has lovingly gifted you with these nine beautifully wrapped presents. Why would you choose to open only one?

In this section, you are encouraged to embark on a journey through all nine Enneagram energies, to explore the connections to your wings, lines, and arrows, as well as the points that may not be part of your primary access. It's important to remember that you always have access to all nine energies, and sometimes, it takes a more deliberate effort to unearth these connections. Embrace this exploration with an open heart, for it's a step toward a deeper understanding of your authentic, multifaceted self, filled with infinite possibilities.

Grounding Meditation

As I move into self-reflection and internal exploration,
I will meditate on these prompts and gently notice
what comes up as I breathe into stillness.

I am ready to begin with three cleansing breaths.

I am inhaling into expansiveness and exhaling constriction.

I have the gift of all nine Enneagram energies within me.

I can freely explore my energy at all nine points.

I am not limited by my type.

I acknowledge my energy and connection to point Three and
point Nine and utilize them for growth and awareness.

I can freely access my wings at point Five and point Seven.

THE BODY CENTER: 8-9-1

In the Body Center, we gain access to our body's wisdom and gut intuition. The Body Center energy is focused on action—affecting the world or environment to avoid being influenced, controlled, or limited by it, and expressing anger or rage in different ways.

What does it look like for me to access
the energies within the Body Center?

Eight

_____

_____

_____

_____

_____

Nine

_____

_____

_____

_____

_____

One

_____

_____

_____

_____

_____

THE HEART CENTER: 2-3-4

In the Heart Center, we gain access to our capacity for emotional honesty and human connection. The Heart Center energy is focused on emotions, self-image, and value—determining your identity and the value you place on your identity plays a key role in how you access the Heart Center energy.

What does it look like for me to access the
energies within the Heart Center?

Two

_____

_____

_____

_____

_____

Three

_____

_____

_____

_____

_____

Four

_____

_____

_____

_____

_____

The Head Center: 5-6-7

In the Head Center, we gain access to our ability to reflect, process, and internalize information. The wisdom we have access to in the Head Center energies allows us to cultivate the space we need for objectivity and inner guidance.

What does it look like for me to access the
energies within the Head Center?

Five

_____
_____
_____
_____
_____

Six

_____
_____
_____
_____
_____

Seven

_____
_____
_____
_____
_____

Do I face any challenges when connecting to particular
Enneagram energies? Can I explore this further?

_____

_____

_____

_____

_____

_____

_____

_____

_____

_____

_____

_____

_____

_____

_____

_____

_____

_____

_____

_____

_____

Reflecting on the connection to my Five wing, how can Five energy bring me the guidance and focus I need to be able to make decisions and find clear solutions to the challenges I face?

_____

_____

_____

_____

_____

_____

_____

_____

_____

_____

_____

_____

_____

_____

_____

_____

_____

_____

_____

_____

The purpose of life, after all, is to live it, to taste experience to the utmost, to reach out eagerly and without fear for newer and richer experiences.

ELEANOR ROOSEVELT

Reflecting on the connection to my Seven wing, how can Seven energy bring me the optimism and joy I need to stay engaged in the present moment?

The secret to happiness is freedom.
And the secret to freedom is courage.

THUCYDIDES

At point Six, I share a connection to point Three, which provides an opportunity to explore the gifts and challenges of this energy. On the upside, this energy can help me find the confidence and courage I need to develop trust in myself and in others and take action to make things happen. On the downside, this energy can narrow my focus, lead to narcissistic tendencies, and create feelings of overwhelm. How have I experienced Three energy in my life?

_____

_____

_____

_____

_____

_____

_____

_____

_____

_____

_____

_____

_____

_____

_____

_____

_____

_____

_____

_____

The best way to find out if you
can trust somebody is to trust them.

ERNEST HEMINGWAY

What does it look like when I tap into the outgoing and charismatic energy at point Three? How does my connection to point Three affect my actions, behaviors, and beliefs?

_____

_____

_____

_____

_____

_____

_____

_____

_____

_____

_____

_____

_____

_____

_____

_____

_____

_____

_____

_____

_____

_____

_____

_____

We are formed and molded by our thoughts.
Those whose minds are shaped by selfless
thoughts give joy when they speak or act.

BUDDHA

At point Six, I share a connection to point Nine, which provides an opportunity to explore the gifts and challenges of this energy. On the upside, this energy can allow me to become focused and grounded in my ability to stay present. On the downside, this energy can lead to feelings of apathy and detachment. How have I experienced Nine energy in my life?

_____

_____

_____

_____

_____

_____

_____

_____

_____

_____

_____

_____

_____

_____

_____

_____

_____

_____

_____

_____

_____

Today, I choose awareness. I choose to be aware of the beauty of life and living. I choose to be aware of the simple pleasures in life. I choose awareness of joy, awareness of peace, and awareness of love.

IYANLA VANZANT

What does it look like when I am able to channel the harmony and grounded energy at point Nine? How does my connection to point Nine affect my actions, behaviors, and beliefs?

_____

_____

_____

_____

_____

_____

_____

_____

_____

_____

_____

_____

_____

_____

_____

_____

_____

_____

_____

_____

_____

_____

_____
_____
_____
_____
_____
_____
_____
_____
_____
_____
_____
_____
_____
_____
_____
_____
_____
_____
_____
_____
_____

Challenges are gifts that force us to search for a new center of gravity. Don't fight them. Just find a new way to stand.

OPRAH WINFREY

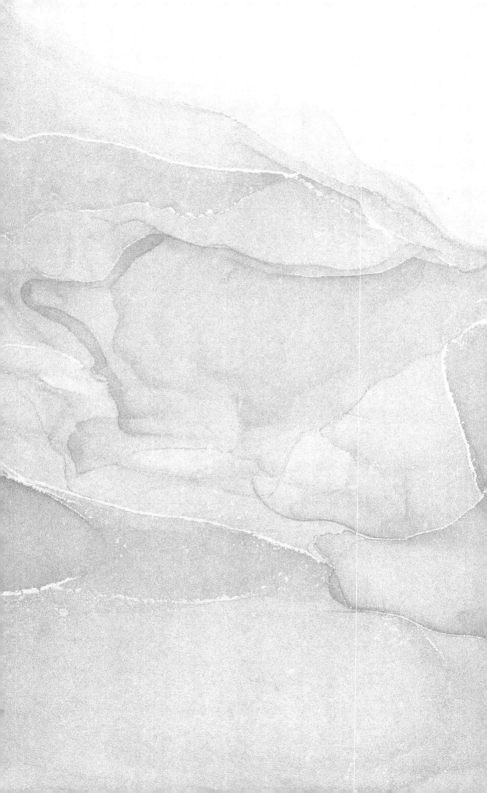

Resources for
CONTINUED EXPLORATION

If you would like to continue your Enneagram journey,
we invite you to visit our resources hub at:

DEBORAHEGERTON.COM/RESOURCES

and explore all of the resources we have gathered for you.
This resource hub is updated frequently, so make sure you
check back when you feel the need for a little inspiration.

You are also encouraged to read my books:

*Know Justice Know Peace: A Transformative Journey of Social Justice,
Anti-Racism, and Healing through the Power of the Enneagram*

*Enneagram Made Easy: Explore the Nine Personality Types of the
Enneagram to Open Your Heart, Find Joy, and Discover Your True Self*

**For easy access to the resources hub, use
your smartphone to scan this QR code:**

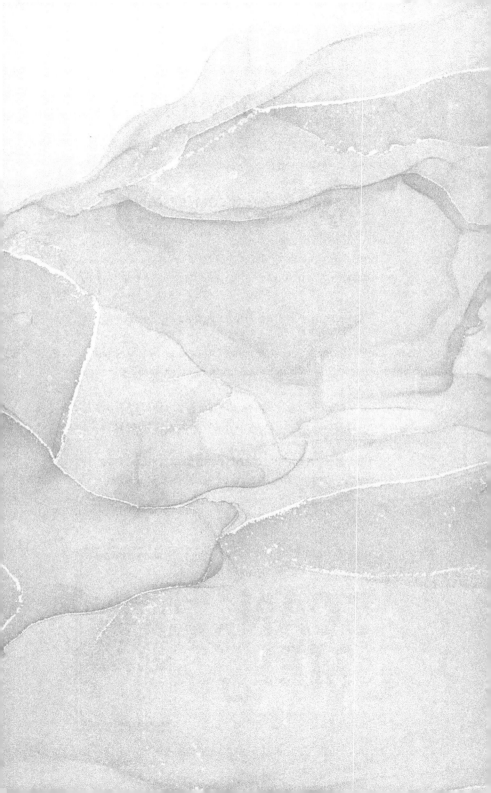

ABOUT THE AUTHOR

Deborah Threadgill Egerton, Ph.D., is an internationally respected psychotherapist, best-selling author, certified Enneagram teacher, unity and belonging advocate for the healing of humanity, consultant, coach, and spiritual teacher. Dr. Egerton specializes in working with the Enneagram to facilitate intentional change in individuals and organizations.

Affectionately referred to as "Dr. E," she has attained IEA Certification with Distinction for her groundbreaking utilization of the Enneagram in the realm of humanitarian healing. Her work is dedicated to dismantling marginalization and transcending the divisive practice of "othering," offering a guiding path toward the harmonious unification of our global community through the transformative forces of kindness and compassion. Dr. E serves as the president of the International Enneagram Association, the global entity responsible for educating, certifying, and accrediting practitioners, teachers, and schools. In her tenure with the IEA, she has been instrumental in fostering an environment of greater inclusivity and accessibility within the global Enneagram community. Her unwavering commitment to justice, equity, diversity, and inclusion has earned her the affectionate title of "Enneagram JEDI" among her peers.

Dr. E extends her coaching and mentoring expertise to a diverse spectrum of individuals, including best-selling authors, top-tier executives, spiritual luminaries, accomplished therapists, and a myriad of coaches, each hailing from distinct and varied backgrounds. For more than two decades, her work has focused on guiding humanity toward a deeper and more compassionate approach to inner work by harnessing the insights of the Enneagram. Her innovative approach to using the Enneagram in social justice and anti-racism work created a blueprint to reconnect people across all dimensions of diversity and has been implemented in various organizations and entities across the globe. She focuses her work on individuals and organizations to help them release false historical narratives and open their minds and hearts to a more compassionate and connected approach to life.

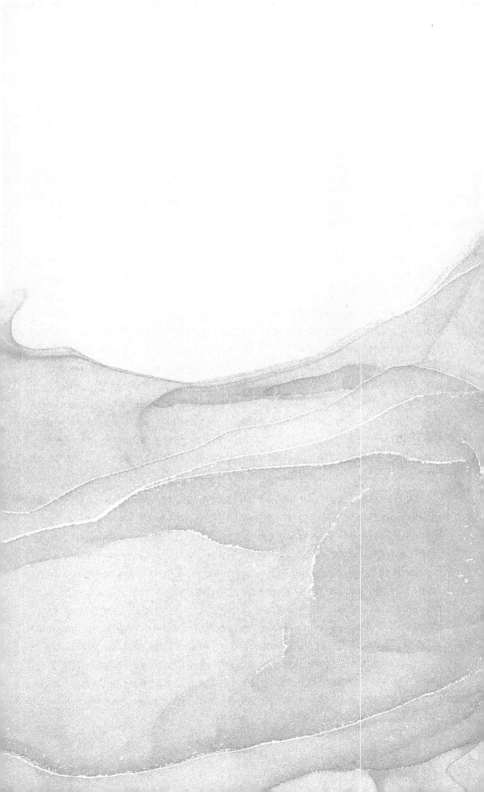

We hope you enjoyed this Hay House book. If you'd like to receive our online catalog featuring additional information on Hay House books and products, or if you'd like to find out more about the Hay Foundation, please contact:

Hay House LLC, P.O. Box 5100, Carlsbad, CA 92018-5100
(760) 431-7695 or (800) 654-5126
www.hayhouse.com® • www.hayfoundation.org

———

Published in Australia by:
Hay House Australia Publishing Pty Ltd
18/36 Ralph St., Alexandria NSW 2015
Phone: +61 (02) 9669 4299
www.hayhouse.com.au

Published in the United Kingdom by:
Hay House UK Ltd
The Sixth Floor, Watson House,
54 Baker Street, London W1U 7BU
Phone: +44 (0) 203 927 7290
www.hayhouse.co.uk

Published in India by:
Hay House Publishers (India) Pvt Ltd
Muskaan Complex, Plot No. 3,
B-2, Vasant Kunj, New Delhi 110 070
Phone: +91 11 41761620
www.hayhouse.co.in

———

Access New Knowledge.
Anytime. Anywhere.

Learn and evolve at your own pace
with the world's leading experts.

www.hayhouseU.com